best wishes!

PRESENTED TO:

....

FROM:

....

© Care for the Family

First published in 2024 by Care for the Family.
Rob Parsons has asserted his right under the Copyright, Designs
and Patents Act 1988 to be identified as the author of this work.

All rights reserved. No part of this publication may be reproduced or
transmitted in any form or by any means, electronic or mechanical,
including photocopying, recording, or any information storage and
retrieval system, without permission in writing from the publisher.

A catalogue record for this book is available from the British Library.

ISBN: 978-1-7397407-9-5

Illustrations, design, and typesetting by Andrew Gordon.
Printed and bound by Xpedient Print Services.

Care for the Family is a Christian initiative to strengthen family life,
offering support for everyone.
A registered charity (England and Wales: 1066905;
Scotland: SC038497).
A company limited by guarantee no. 3482910.
Registered in England and Wales.
Registered office: Tovey House, Cleppa Park, Newport, NP10 8BA.

DEDICATION

To everyone who has left a light on ...

ACKNOWLEDGEMENTS

Many thanks to Jess Hills, Stephen Hayes, Sarah Rowlands,
and Esther Holt for all of their hard work in creating
this very special book.

Always
leave a light
on

ROB PARSONS

I wonder if there may come a time in your life when you feel you've really blown it and there's no way back.

Maybe that's already happened for you,
and you've not yet found your way home.

Or maybe you're the one peering out through the gap in the curtains, waiting for a knock at the front door that feels like it will never come.

If any of this sounds like you,
I want to invite you to consider
a story that Jesus told.

It has become one of the best-known
pieces of prose in the world.

In fact, when I was studying
English Literature, my lecturer
*(who told us quite clearly that
she was 'not religious at all')*
said that she thought this
little parable was perhaps
the greatest short story
ever written.

It's about a father who had two children.

Now if you ever become a parent and
have more than one child, you may well
find that your offspring have entirely
different personalities and characteristics.

Often you will find that one will be
perfectly behaved and the other
will test you on a daily basis.

The two boys in this story are like that.

It is often called the 'Parable of the Prodigal Son', but actually it is a story about both children: one compliant and well behaved, the other a hell-raiser.

The second brother asks for his share of his father's estate and leaves home as fast as he can. While he is partying, his older brother works diligently in the father's business.

But then the younger brother falls on hard times – he ends up penniless and friendless.

And at the moment when he is at his lowest, he thinks again of home …

... and decides to start the
long
walk
back.

Of course, he has no idea how his father, whose heart he has broken, will receive him, so he prepares a speech which, in essence, asks if he can work for bed and breakfast until he gets on his feet.

What he doesn't know is that every day since he left, his father has been looking down the road ...

... and waiting.

Some years ago, a woman wrote to me and said that when her daughter was eighteen, she had walked out of their home after a row.

She didn't get in touch, and they didn't know whether she was alive or dead.

At night, as this mother and her husband turned off the lights before they went to bed, she would always say to him,

'Leave the porch light on.'

And every Christmas she would put a little Christmas tree in the front of the house, its lights shining, just as she used to when her daughter was a child.

That couple didn't see
their daughter for six years.

Then one day, out of the blue,
she knocked on their door...

... and fell into her mother's arms.

She said:

'Mum, I so often wanted to come home,
but I was too ashamed. But sometimes,
in the early hours of the morning,
I would drive my car into our street
and just sit there.

I used to gaze at the houses and every
one of them was dark apart from our
house:

You *always* left a light on.

And at Christmas I would do the same:
just sit there in the darkness and look at
the Christmas tree you had put outside.

I knew it was for me.'

The parent in the old story is not
so different from that mother.

When the 'prodigal' son is *way*
down the road, the father sees him
and starts running towards him.

The son tries to get his speech out,
but the father just won't let him –
he is hugging him so hard the boy
can hardly breathe.

And then,
the older brother comes on the scene.

He is judgemental, bitter, and with
no shortage of vitriol for the father:

'Why are we throwing a party for *him*?

He has wasted your money and his life.'

What he doesn't know is that his
father can't help himself; he loves
his son so much that the past
doesn't matter right now.

All that matters …
is that his boy is home.

He says: 'Your brother was dead and he's alive
again. He was lost and is found.'

The father doesn't leave the older brother sulking out in the cold. He urges him to join in the celebrations.

But the son refuses.

The sad truth is that one of his boys had been lost away from home, but the other is still lost at home.

Perhaps this tale of love, acceptance and forgiveness really is the greatest short story ever told.

In my book *The Wisdom House*, which I wrote for my grandchildren, I told them about this incredible parable.

And I said: 'I want you to know that whatever you do, you can always come home.

If your mum and dad are alive, I'm sure they'll run down that road towards you, and certainly if I'm still about I'll whiz towards you on my Zimmer frame.

But even if, for any reason, we are not there – another father will be waiting.

And there will always be a light on.'

About Care for the Family

Established in 1988, Care for the Family is a charity based in the UK, but with an increasing reach internationally. Our aim is to support families whatever their circumstances. We provide this support, online and in person, for parents, couples and those who are bereaved, through events, courses, podcasts, volunteer befrienders, books, and other evidence-based, accessible resources. We also train those who work with families whether in a professional or informal capacity.

The Wisdom House

You'll find this story and many more in
The Wisdom House by Rob Parsons.

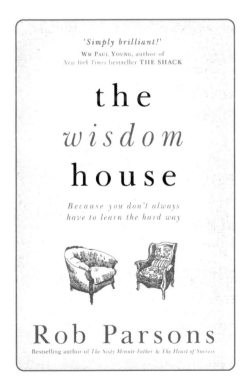

ISBN: 978-1-444-74566-5